Distributed by

Publishers / New York

A DIVISION OF GROSSET & DUNLAP

SPECIAL BOOK CLUB EDITION

CONTENTS

IF WISHES WERE HORSES

If wishes were horses,
Beggars would ride;
If turnips were watches,
I'd wear one by my side.

YANKEE DOODLE

Yankee Doodle went to town,
Riding on a pony;
Stuck a feather in his hat,
And called it Macaroni.

RIDE A COCK-HORSE

Ride a cock-horse to Banbury Cross,
To see a fine lady upon a white horse;
Rings on her fingers and bells on her toes,
She shall have music wherever she goes.

MARY HAD A LITTLE LAMB

Mary had a little lamb,
Its fleece was white as snow;
And everywhere that Mary went,
The lamb was sure to go.

It followed her to school one day,
Which was against the rule;
It made the children laugh and pla
To see a lamb at school.

LITTLE MAID, PRETTY MAI

Little maid, pretty maid, whithe
  go thou?
"Down in the meadow to milk
  my cow."
Shall I go with thee? "No, not
  now;
When I send for thee, then come
  thou."

LITTLE BO-PEEP

Little Bo-Peep has lost her she
And can't tell where to find
  them;
Leave them alone, and they'll
  come home,
Wagging their tails behind
  them.

DEEDLE, DEEDLE DUMPLING

Deedle, deedle, dumpling, my son John,
He went to bed with his stockings on;
One shoe off, and one shoe on,
Deedle, deedle, dumpling, my son John.

BAA, BAA, BLACK SHEEP

Baa baa, black sheep,
　　have you any wool?
Yes, sir, yes, sir, three bags full;
One for my master,
　　one for my dame,
And one for the little boy
　　who lives down the lane.

HANDY PANDY

Handy Pandy, Jack-a-dandy,
Loves plum cake and sugar candy;
He bought some at the grocer's shop;
And out he came, hop, hop, hop!

BLOW, WIND, BLOW!

Blow, wind, blow! and go, mill go!
That the miller may grind his corn
That the baker may take it,
And into rolls make it,
And send us some hot in the morn.

THIRTY DAYS HATH
SEPTEMBER

Thirty days hath September,
April, June, and November.
February has twenty-eight alone
All the rest have thirty-one;
But Leap Year coming once
    in four,
February then has one day more

THE WINDS

The south wind brings
    wet weather,
The north wind wet and
    cold together,
The west wind always
    brings us rain,
The east wind blows
    it back again.

LITTLE MISS MUFFET

Little Miss Muffet,
Sat on a tuffet,
Eating her curds and whey;

Along came a spider,
And sat down beside her,
And frightened Miss Muffet away.

MOLLY, MY SISTER, AND
I FELL OUT

Molly, my sister, and I fell out,
And what do you think it was
   all about?
She loved coffee and I loved tea,
And that was the reason we
   couldn't agree.

ONE, TWO, BUCKLE
MY SHOE

One, two, buckle my shoe;
Three, four, shut the door;
Five, six, pick up sticks;
Seven, eight, lay them straight;
Nine, ten, a big fat hen.

H. HOBBIE

HUSH-A-BYE, BABY

Hush-a-bye, baby, on the tree top!
When the wind blows the cradle will rock
When the bough breaks the cradle will fa
Down will come baby, cradle and all.

THE CUCKOO

The cuckoo comes in April
Stops all the month of May
Sings a song at midsumme
And then he goes away.

ROCK-A-BYE, BABY, THY CRADLE IS GREEN

Rock-a-bye baby, thy cradle is green;
Father's a nobleman, mother's a queen;
Betty's a lady, and wears a gold ring;
Johnny's a drummer, and drums for the King.

HERE WE GO

Here we go up, up, up;
Here we go down, down, down;
Here we go backward
 and forward;
And here we go round,
 round, round.

SALLY GO ROUND
THE SUN

Sally go round the sun,
Sally go round the moon,
Sally go round the chimney pots,
On a Saturday afternoon.

THE MULBERRY BUSH

Here we go round the mulberry bush,
The mulberry bush, the mulberry bush;

Here we go round the mulberry bush,
On a cold and frosty morning.

THERE'S A NEAT LITTLE CLOCK

There's a neat little clock,
In the schoolroom it stands,
And it points to the time,
With its two little hands.

And may we, like the clock,
Keep a face clean and brigh
With hands ever ready,
To do what is right.

HICKORY, DICKORY, DOC

Hickory, dickory, dock!
The mouse ran up the cloc
The clock struck one, and
    down he run,
Hickory, dickory, dock!

MISTRESS MARY, QUITE CONTRARY

Mistress Mary, quite contrary,
How does your garden grow?

With silver bells, and cockleshells,
And pretty maids all in a row.

PLY THE SPADE

Ply the spade,
And ply the hoe,
Plant the seed,
And it will grow.

ONE MISTY, MOISTY MORNING

One misty, moisty morning,
When cloudy was the weather;
I chanced to meet an old man,
Clothed all in leather.

He began to compliment,
And I began to grin;
How do you do, and how do you do?
And how do you do again?

RAIN, RAIN, GO AWAY

Rain, rain, go away,
Come again another day;
Little Johnny wants to play.

A SUNSHINY SHOWER

A sunshiny shower,
Won't last half an hour.

DOCTOR FOSTER

Doctor Foster went to Gloucester,
In a shower of rain;
He stepped in a puddle up to his middle,
And never went there again.

THE LITTLE BIRD

Once I saw a little bird
Come hop, hop, hop;
So I cried, "Little bird,
Will you stop, stop, stop?"

I was going to the window
To say, "How do you do?"
But he shook his little tail,
And far away he flew.

PUSSYCAT

"Pussycat, pussycat,
Where have you been?"
"I've been to London
To visit the Queen."

"Pussycat, pussycat,
What did you there?"
"I frightened a little mouse
Under her chair."

I LOVE LITTLE PUSSY

I love little Pussy,
Her coat is so warm;
And if I don't hurt her,
She'll do me no harm.

I'll sit by the fire,
And give her some food;
And Pussy will love me,
Because I am good.

OLD MOTHER HUBBARD

Old Mother Hubbard,
Went to the cupboard,
To get her poor dog a bone;
When she got there,
The cupboard was bare,
And so the poor dog had none.

PAT A CAKE

Pat a cake, pat a cake,
  Baker's man.
Bake me a cake,
  As fast as you can.
Pat it and prick it,
  And mark it with a B,
And put it in the oven
  For Baby and me.

POLLY, PUT THE KETTLE ON

Polly, put the kettle on,
Polly, put the kettle on,
Polly, put the kettle on,
We'll all have tea.

Sukey, take it off again,
Sukey, take it off again,
Sukey, take it off again,
They've all gone away.

21

GEORGIE PORGIE, PUDDING AND PIE

Georgie Porgie, pudding and pie,
Kissed the girls and made them cry;
When the boys came out to play,
Georgie Porgie ran away.

LITTLE BOY BLUE

Little Boy Blue, come blow your
  horn,
The sheep's in the meadow, the
  cow's in the corn;
But where is the little boy who
  looks after the sheep?
He's under the haystack fast
  asleep.
Will you wake him? No, not I!
For if I do, he's sure to cry.

HICKETY PICKETY, MY BLACK HEN

Hickety Pickety, my black hen,
She lays eggs for gentlemen.
Gentlemen come every day,
To see what my black hen
  doth lay;
Sometimes nine, and sometimes
  ten,
Hickety Pickety, my fat hen.

TIME TO RISE

A birdie with a yellow bill,
Hopped upon the windowsill,
Cocked his shining eye and said,
"Ain't you 'shamed, you sleepyhead?"

LAZY MARY

Lazy Mary, will you get up,
Will you get up, will you get up,
Lazy Mary, will you get up,
Will you get up today?

No, no, mother, I won't get up,
I won't get up, I won't get up,
No, no, mother, I won't get up,
I won't get up today!

COCK CROWS IN THE MORN

Cock crows in the morn,
  to tell us to rise;
And he who lies late,
  will never be wise.
For early to bed,
  and early to rise,
Is the way to be
  healthy, wealthy and wise.

23

RING A RING O' ROSES

Ring a ring o' roses,
A pocketful of posies.
Tisha! Tisha!
We all fall down.

LITTLE GIRL, LITTLE GIRL

"Little girl, little girl, where
  have you been?"
"Gathering roses to give to the
  Queen."

"Little girl, little girl, what
  gave she you?"
"She gave me a diamond as big
  as my shoe."

WHERE ARE YOU GOING, MY PRETTY MAID?

"Where are you going, my pretty maid?"
"I'm going a-milking, sir," she said.
"May I go with you, my pretty maid?"
"You're kindly welcome, sir," she said.

"What is your father, my pretty maid?"
"My father's a farmer, sir," she said.
"What is your fortune, my pretty maid?"
"My face is my fortune, sir," she said.

"Then I can't marry you, my pretty maid!"
"Nobody asked you, sir!" she said.

LOVELY RAINBOW

Lovely rainbow hung so high,
Quite across the distant sky;
Please touch the ground close by my side,
And o'er your bridge I'll pony ride.

WHEN I WAS A LITTLE GIRL

When I was a little girl,
About seven years old,
I had not a petticoat,
To keep me from the cold.

So I went to Darlington,
That pretty little town,
And there I bought a petticoat,
A cloak and a gown.

CURLY LOCKS

Curly Locks, Curly Locks,
Wilt thou be mine?
Thou shalt not wash dishes,
Nor yet feed the swine;
But sit on a cushion,
And sew a fine seam,
And feed upon strawberries,
Sugar and cream.

MONDAY'S CHILD

Monday's child is fair of face,
Tuesday's child is full of grace,

Wednesday's child is full of woe,
Thursday's child has far to go,

Friday's child is loving and givin
Saturday's child works hard
  for its living;

And a child that is born
  on the Sabbath day,
Is fair, and wise,
  and good, and gay.

THREE LITTLE KITTENS

Three little kittens, they lost
  their mittens,
And they began to cry,
"Oh, mother, dear, we greatly
  fear,
That we have lost our mittens."

"What! lost your mittens, you
  naughty kittens!
Then you shall have no pie."
"Meow, meow, meow,
  meow,
Then we shall have no pie."

WHO'S THAT RINGING AT OUR FRONT DOOR BELL?

"Who's that ringing at our front
  door bell?"
"I'm a little pussycat and I'm not
  very well."

"Then put your little nose in a
  little mutton fat,
And that's the way to cure a little
  pussycat."

JOHN AND JANE

As John and Jane walked through the lane,
One very pleasant Sunday,
Said John to Jane, "Unless it rain,
Tomorrow will be Monday."

ONE, TWO, THREE, FOUR

One, two, three, four and five,
I caught a hare alive;
Six, seven, eight, nine, ten,
I let him go again.

TWO PIGEONS

I had two pigeons bright and gay,
They flew from me the other day.
What was the reason they did go?
I cannot tell, for I do not know.

WHISTLE, DAUGHTER

"Whistle, daughter, whistle;
Whistle, daughter, dear."
"I cannot whistle, Mummy,
I cannot whistle clear."
"Whistle, daughter, whistle;
Whistle for a pound."
"I cannot whistle, Mummy,
I cannot make a sound."

TWO BLACKBIRDS

There were two blackbirds
Sitting on a hill,
The one named Jack,
The other named Jill.
Fly away Jack!
Fly away Jill!
Come again Jack!
Come again Jill!

BYE, BABY BUNTING

Bye, Baby Bunting,
Daddy's gone a-hunting,
To get a little rabbit's skin,
To wrap his Baby Bunting in.

RIDE, BABY, RIDE

Ride, baby, ride,
Pretty baby shall ride,
And have a little puppy dog
  tied to her side,
And little pussycat
  tied to the other.
And away she shall ride
  to see her grandmother,
To see her grandmother,
To see her grandmother.

COME, MY CHILDREN

Come, my children, come away,
For the sun shines bright today;
Little children, come with me,
Birds and brooks and posies see;
Get your hats and come away,
For it is a pleasant day.

Everything is laughing, singing,
All the pretty flowers are springing;
See the kitten full of fun,
Sporting in the brilliant sun;
Children, too, may sport and play,
For it is a pleasant day.

I'M GLAD THE SKY IS PAINTED BLUE

I'm glad the sky is painted blue,
And earth is painted green;
With such a lot of nice fresh air,
All sandwiched in between.

THE DOVE SAYS

The dove says, "Coo, coo, what shall I do?
I can scarce maintain two."
"Pooh! Pooh!" says the wren. "I have got ten,
And I keep them all like gentlemen."

A LITTLE COCK SPARROW

A little cock sparrow sat on a
  green tree,
And he chirruped, he chirruped,
  so merry was he.

JENNY WREN

Jenny Wren last week was wed,
And built her nest in
  grandpa's shed;
Look next week and you
  shall see,
Two little eggs, and maybe three.

HERE AM I

Here am I,
Little jumping Joan,
When nobody's with me,
I'm always alone.

BRING OUT THE CARRIAGE

Bring out the carriage, exactly at five,
We'll all go riding and Harry shall drive;
The little dog Tracy shall run by our side,
And when he is tired may jump in and ride.

WOULDN'T IT BE FUNNY?

Wouldn't it be funny,
Wouldn't it, now,
If the dog said, "Moo"
And the cow said, "Bow-wow?"
If the cat sang and whistled,
And the bird said, "Meow?"
Wouldn't it be funny,
Wouldn't it, now?

DAFFY-DOWN-DILLY

Daffy-down-dilly has come
    up to town,
In a yellow petticoat and a
    green gown.

MARCH WINDS

March winds and April
  showers,
Bring forth May flowers.

LITTLE WIND

Little wind, blow on the hill top;
Little wind, blow down the plain;
Little wind, blow up the sunshine;
Little wind, blow off the rain.

WHO HAS SEEN THE WIND

Who has seen the wind?
Neither you nor I;
But when the trees bow down their heads,
The wind is passing by.

LITTLE MAIDEN

Little maiden, better tarry;
Time enough next year to marry.
Hearts may change,
And so may fancy;
Wait a little longer, Nancy.

SUMMER BREEZE

Summer breeze, so softly blowing,
In my garden pinks are growing;
If you go and send the showers,
You may come and smell my flowers.

MOTHER, MAY I GO OUT
TO SWIM?

Mother, may I go out to swim?
Yes, my darling daughter.
Hang your clothes on a hickory limb,
But don't go near the water.

HOT CROSS BUNS!

Hot cross buns! Hot cross buns!
One a penny, two a penny,
    Hot cross buns!
If you have no daughters,
Give them to your sons,
One a penny, two a penny,
    Hot cross buns!
But if you have none of these
    little elves,
Then you may eat them all
    yourselves.

LITTLE TOMMY TUCKER

Little Tommy Tucker,
Sings for his supper.
What shall he eat?
White bread and butter.

How will he cut it,
Without e'er a knife?
How can he marry,
Without e'er a wife?

JACK SPRAT

Jack Sprat could eat no fat,
His wife could eat no lean;
And so betwixt them both,
    you see,
They licked the platter clean.

OLD MOTHER GOOSE

Old Mother Goose when
She wanted to wander,

Would ride through the air
On a very fine gander.

UP IS THE SUN

Come, my dear children,
Up is the sun;
Birds are all singing,
And morn has begun.

Up from the bed, Miss,
Out on the lea;
The horses are waiting,
For you and for me!

TO MARKET, TO MARKET

To market, to market, to buy a
 fat pig,
Home again, home again,
 jiggety jig;
To market, to market, to buy a
 fat hog,
Home again, home again,
 jiggety jog.

BOBBY SHAFTOE'S GONE TO SEA

Bobby Shaftoe's gone to sea,
Silver buckles on his knee;
He'll come back and marry me,
Pretty Bobby Shaftoe!

Bobby Shaftoe's fat and fair,
Combing down his yellow hair;
He's my love for evermore,
Pretty Bobby Shaftoe!

WHAT ARE LITTLE GIRLS MADE OF?

What are little girls made of?
What are little girls made of?
Sugar and spice and everything nice,
That's what little girls are made of.

WHAT ARE LITTLE BOYS MADE OF?

What are little boys made of?
What are little boys made of?
Frogs and snails, and puppy dogs' tails,
And that's what little boys are made of!

JACK AND JILL

Jack and Jill,
Went up the hill,
To fetch a pail of water;
Jack fell down,
And broke his crown,
And Jill came tumbling after.

Then up Jack got,
And home did trot,
As fast as he could caper;
They put him to bed,
And plastered his head,
With vinegar and brown paper.

"BOW-WOW," SAYS THE DOG

"Bow-wow," says the dog;
"Mew, mew," says the cat;
"Grunt, grunt," goes the hog;
And "Squeak," says the rat.

"To-woo," says the owl;
"Caw, caw," goes the crow;
"Quack, quack," goes the duck;
And "Moo," says the cow.

BOW-WOW-WOW

Bow-wow-wow,
Whose dog are thou?
Little Tommy Tinker's dog,
Bow-wow-wow!

OH WHERE, OH WHERE HAS MY LITTLE DOG GONE?

Oh where, oh where has my
   little dog gone?
Oh where, oh where can
   he be?
With his ears cut short and his
   tail cut long,
Oh where, oh where is he?

HOLLY HOBBIE

THE NORTH WIND

The north wind doth blow,
And we shall have snow,
And what will the robin do
   then, poor thing?
He'll sit in the barn
And keep himself warm,
And hide his head under his
   wing, poor thing!

FINIKIN, WINIKIN WO

Finikin, winikin wo,
I think we shall have some snow;
And Charley and Ned
Must have a new sled,
Finikin, winikin wo!

SING A SONG OF SIXPENCE

Sing a song of sixpence, a pocket full of rye;
Four-and-twenty blackbirds baked in a pie.
When the pie was opened, the birds began to sing;
Wasn't that a dainty dish to set before the King?

The King was in the counting-house, counting out
   his money;
The Queen was in the parlour, eating bread and honey.
The maid was in the garden, hanging out the clothes;
When down came a little bird and snapped off her nose!

ROSES ARE RED

Roses are red,
Violets are blue;
Sugar is sweet,
And so are you.

LITTLE FOLKS

Little folks, little folks,
Now then for bed!
A pillow is waiting,
For each little head.

Sleep all the night,
And wake in the morn;
Robert shall sound
The call on his horn.